spot

HOLIDAYS

DIWALI

by Mari Schuh

AMICUS | AMICUS INK

lamps

sweets

Look for these words and pictures as you read.

rangoli

fireworks

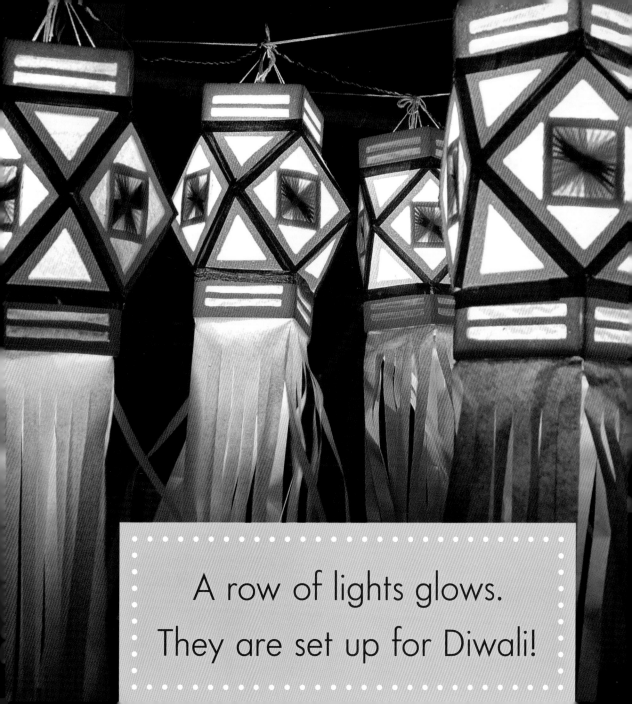

A row of lights glows.
They are set up for Diwali!

Diwali is the Hindu New Year.
It's in October or November.
It's called the festival of lights.

lamps

See the clay lamps?
They are diyas.
They burn oil.

See the rangoli?
It's made of flower petals.
It brings good luck.

rangoli

sweets

See the sweets?
Many treats are eaten.
Yum!

See the fireworks?

Boom!

They light up the sky.

fireworks

People give gifts. They pray.
A new year is here!

lamps

See the clay lamps?
They are diyas.
They burn oil.

sweets

See the sweets?
Many treats are eaten.
Yum!

lamps

sweets

Did you find?

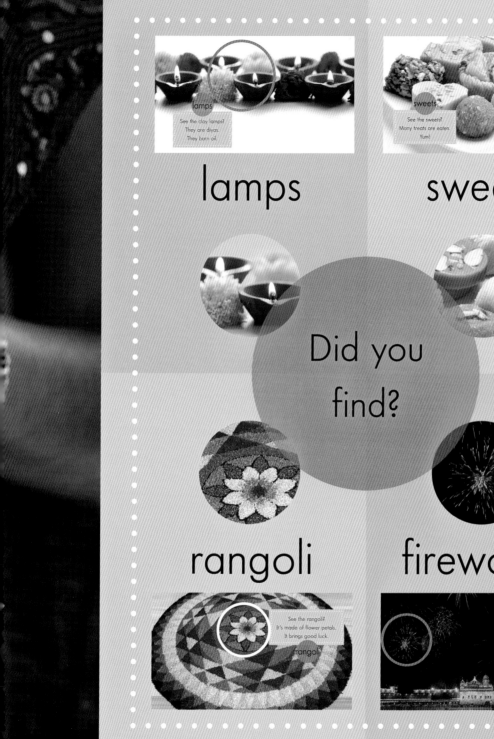

rangoli

fireworks

See the rangoli?
It's made of flower petals.
It brings good luck.

rangoli

See the fireworks?
Boom!
They light up the sky.

fireworks

Spot is published by Amicus and Amicus Ink
P.O. Box 1329, Mankato, MN 56002
www.amicuspublishing.us

Library of Congress Cataloging-in-Publication Data
Names: Schuh, Mari C., 1975- author.
Title: Diwali / by Mari Schuh.
Description: Mankato, Minnesota : Amicus/Amicus Ink,
  [2020] | Series: Spot holidays | Audience: Grades: K-3.
Identifiers: LCCN 2018047347 (print) | LCCN 2019013568
  (ebook) | ISBN 9781681518428 (pdf) | ISBN
  9781681518022 (library binding) | ISBN
  9781681525303 (pbk.)
Subjects: LCSH: Divali--Juvenile literature. | Fasts and feasts-
  -Hinduism--Juvenile literature. | Picture puzzles--Juvenile
  literature.
Classification: LCC BL1239.82.D58 (ebook) | LCC BL1239.82.
  D58 S354 2020 (print) | DDC 294.5/36--dc23
LC record available at https://lccn.loc.gov/2018047347

Printed in China

HC 10 9 8 7 6 5 4 3 2 1
PB 10 9 8 7 6 5 4 3 2 1

Alissa Thielges, editor
Deb Miner, series designer
Veronica Scott, book designer
Holly Young and Shane Freed,
  photo researchers

Photos by Getty/Clandy-Images
cover, 16; Alamy/Subodh Sathe 1;
Shutterstock/Soumitra Pendse 3;
Shutterstock/India Picture 4–5; Alamy/
Anshu A 6–7; iStock/DBhakta 8–9;
iStock/highviews 10–11; Alamy/Sourabh
Gandhi 12–13; Shutterstock/Wong Yu
Liang 14–15

DIWALI